UFO SHAPE	BOTTOM VIEW	BOTTOM ANGLE		SIDE VIEW	
		A	B	A	B
1. FLAT DISC A. 10-1-4 Cox 7-7-52 Newhouse B. 7-9-47 Johnson 7-14-52 Nash		oval		*lens-shaped*	*coin-like*
2. DOMED DISC A. 9-21-58 Fitzgerald 4-24-62 Gavelein B. 5-11-50 Trent 8-7-52 Jansen		*hat-shaped*		*World War I helmet*	
3. SATURN DISC (Double dome) A. 10-4-54 Salandin 1-16-58 Trindade 10-2-61 Harris B. 8-20-56 Moore	A B elliptical or *winged oval*	*diamond-shaped*		*Saturn-shaped*	
4. HEMISPHERICAL DISC 4-24-49 Redmond 1-23-61 Pullino 2-7-61 Walley		*parachute*		*mushroom* *half moon*	
5. FLATTENED SPHERE 10-1-48 Gorman 4-27-50 Adickes 10-9-51 C.A.A.					sometimes with peak
6. SPHERICAL (Circular from all angles) 3-45 Delarof 1-20-52 Nailor 10-12-61 Edwards	A metallic-appearing ball	ball of glowing light	B		
7. ELLIPTICAL 12-20-58 Arbiccen 11-2-57 Levelland 8-13-60 Corson	*football* *egg-shaped*				
8. TRIANGULAR 5-7-56 G.O.C. 5-22-60 Majorca				*tear-drop*	
9. CYLINDRICAL (Rocket-like) 8-1-46 Puckett 7-7-59 Chiles	*cigar-shaped*		**10. LIGHT SOURCE ONLY** *star-like* or *planet-like*		

Published by
Walker Publishing Company, Inc., New York
A Division of Bloomsbury Publishing

All papers used by Walker & Company are natural,
recyclable products made from wood grown in well-
managed forests. The manufacturing processes conform to
the environmental regulations of the country of origin.

Library of Congress Cataloging-in-Publication Data
has been applied for.

ISBN: 978-0-8027-7788-1

Visit Walker & Company's Web site
at www.walkerbooks.com

First U.S. edition 2012

1 3 5 7 9 10 8 6 4 2

Designed and typeset by
Wooden Books Ltd, Glastonbury, UK

Printed in the United States of America

UFO

STRANGE SPACE ON EARTH

Paul Whitehead & George Wingfield

Walker & Company
New York

WOODEN
BOOKS

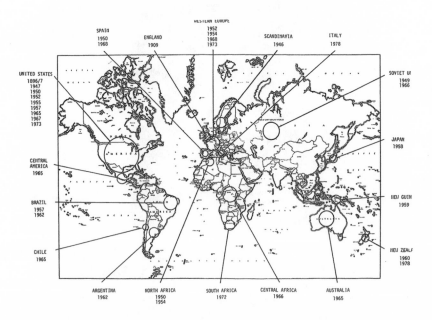

Above: Major UFO flaps across the world during the 20th century.

CONTENTS

Les Soucoupes Volantes viennent d'un autre Monde
Editions
FLEUVE NOIR
JIMMY GUIEU

INTRODUCTION

A UFO, or unidentified flying object, is a mysterious something seen in the sky. In the mid 20th century they were called "flying saucers" (in French *soucoupes volantes*, *see opposite*), or "spaceships" from other worlds, but strange things had been seen in the heavens long before then. In the Middle Ages they were angels or demons, while 18th and 19th century folklore tells of "the little people," elves or fairies, today often interpreted as visitors from another kind of space.

There is no doubt that unidentified objects seen in the sky can turn out to be all sorts of things. Every year thousands of people see unfamiliar aircraft, stars, planets, artificial satellites and even luminous clouds, which they fail to recognize. Yet, while these certainly account for many UFOs, there remain hundreds of others that defy explanation, and it is these encounters that are the subject of this book. We will leave it up to you to ponder their origin, whether mundane, extraterrestrial or interdimensional. Many witnesses, including experienced pilots, say they are driven to believe the UFOs they have seen are "not from here," despite people's disbelief and the damage to their own reputations.

Scientists regularly ponder whether or not our universe may be teeming with life, yet they often struggle to relate this to reliable UFO sightings, a phenomenon almost as strange as the reports they dismiss. The universe seems to be finely tuned to maximize the chances for biological life, yet where evolution eventually leads we do not know. It may well be that some of the mysterious UFOs seen worldwide represent the tip of a UFO reality far stranger than we can possibly imagine. Mind open? Read on ...

HISTORICAL ODDITIES
from cave art to Ezekiel's wheel

From Biblical through to modern times, humans have slowly become aware of the enormous scale of the universe. With squillions of galaxies, suns and planets, it now seems that man may not play the central role. Similar thinking may have been common thousands of years ago among our native ancestors whose conceptual (and possibly drug-induced) cave art ranged from abstractions of shamanic visions to details of daily life. On their walls we see not only animals, but also strange-looking humanoid beings (*see example from Algeria top left opposite*). Are these ancestors? Spirits? Gods? Visitors from the future? Entities from other worlds? Or are they fantasies?

In the ancient Indian Vedas (c. 1500 B.C.), flying chariots of the gods, or *vimanas*, are described in detail (*lower left opposite*), while Babylonian and South American tablets show flying machines (*below*). The Bible contains similar curious objects (*e.g., Ezekiel's Wheel, opposite top right*) and many other flying chariots appear elsewhere in antiquity.

Rock art from Tassili n'Ajjer, southern Algeria, looking like a bizarre "spaceman" circa 5000 B.C.

Above: Ezekiel's close encounter with a wheeled and fiery object which whipped up the dust: "Out of the midst thereof came the likeness of four living creatures with the likeness of a man." The wheels appeared as "a wheel in the middle of a wheel ... they went upon their four sides ... and their rings were full of eyes about."

Above: An illustration of the Shakuna Vimana with hinged wings and tail, drawn in 1923 under instruction of S. Shastry with details from the Vedas.

Above: Roman coin showing a wheel-like disk with portholes in the clouds flying over a landscape.

EARLY FLYING MACHINES
eerie ships in the sky

Records of unidentified flying objects litter medieval records. The Archbishop of Lyons, writing in the 9th century, tells of the French peasantry's belief in a "certain region called Magonia whence come ships in the clouds." The archbishop wrote that he had witnessed the stoning to death of "three men and a woman who said they had fallen from these same ships." In 1211, a similar story was related by Gervase of Tilbury:

> "There happened in the borough of Cloera [Ireland] one Sunday, while the people were at Mass, a marvel. In this town is a church dedicated to St. Kinarus. It befell that an anchor was dropped from the sky, with a rope attached to it, and one of the flukes caught in the arch above the church door. The people rushed out of the church and saw in the sky a ship with men on board, floating before the anchor cable, and they saw a man leap overboard and jump down to the anchor, as if to release it. He looked as if he were swimming in water. The folk rushed up and tried to seize him; but the Bishop forbade the people to hold the man, for it might kill him, he said. The man was freed, and hurried up to the ship, where the crew cut the rope and the ship sailed out of sight..."

Sightings continued in the centuries which followed. Crop circles are first recorded from 1678 (*opposite center left*); a strange red light moving up a mountainside was noted by Dorothy Wordsworth in her *Grasmere Journal*, March 17th, 1802; and the first UFO flaps occur on the eastern seaboard of the U.S.A. in 1887 and 1896–97 (*below*).

Above: Hans Glaser's woodcut of aerial objects above Nuremberg, Germany, April 14th, 1561.

Above: Early Chinese woodcut of a sage with what appears to be a landed spacecraft.

Above: 1678 woodcut of "the mowing devil," from Hertfordshire, an early explanation for crop circles, circular swirled areas of grass or grains.

Above: Ancient North African cave painting depicting something very similar to a UFO.

Above: In the 10th century Tibetan translation of the Sanskrit Prajnaparamita Sutra two hat-like objects float in mid air. One has portholes.

Far left: 19th century sketch of a UFO seen by Angie Till. Near left: Newspaper reporter's sketch of an airship which passed over Nashville in April 1897.

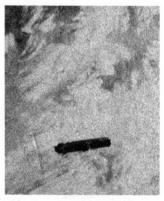

Above: 1870 photo of a cigar-shaped UFO taken from the summit of Mount Washington.

SPACE IS BIG
scary science and the birth of fantasy

A thousand years ago most people thought of themselves as being at the center of quite a small universe. It was only in the 1600s that Kepler and Copernicus proved that we live on a planet orbiting a sun. Then, in 1750 Thomas Wright suggested our solar system was just one of many (*opposite top right*), and in 1785 William Herschel drew the first picture of our galaxy (*opposite top left*).

If there were other worlds, maybe some were like ours! In 1877 Giovanni Schiaparelli drew a map of Mars showing canals (*opposite center*). A few years later, in 1898, with new galaxies full of billions of stars being discovered every week, H. G. Wells published the first popular science fiction book on aliens, *The War of the Worlds*.

Science, fiction and fantasy had merged, and would go on to dominate popular thinking about space, aliens and UFOs right through to the modern day.

Above: William Herschel's 1785 first suggestive drawing of the Milky Way as a distinct galaxy.

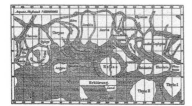

Above: Schiaparelli's map of Martian canals, a vision supported by astronomer Percival Lowell. H. G. Wells' aliens (below) came from Mars.

Above: Thomas Wright's visionary 1750 drawing of unique solar systems inhabiting and filling space. Planets orbiting stars were now the norm.

Above and left: While scientists measured and pondered their results, fantasists and film-makers dreamed up terrifying implications of the science, leaving the public uninformed but entertained.

FLYING SAUCERS
the beginning of the saucer era

On June 24th, 1947 businessman Kenneth Arnold from Idaho was flying east in his private plane over Washington State near Mount Rainier. It was a clear day with excellent visibility. Surprised, first by a very bright flash in the sky and then by another, he looked to the north and saw a formation of nine objects flying south at high speed. These seemingly reflected the sun brilliantly and dipped and rose as they flew together. "They flew like a saucer would if you skipped it across water," he said later. The objects were horseshoe or crescent shaped, flying with the blunt end forward.

His story attracted huge press attention and the description of their flight as being saucer-like led immediately to the appellation "flying saucers." It was the beginning of the flying saucer era.

Within the next few months reports of flying saucers came thick and fast from all over the U.S. There was no reason to doubt the truthfulness of Kenneth Arnold.

Left: Arnold timed the mysterious objects as they flew past Mount Rainier ahead of his plane and then as they passed by Mount Adams roughly 47 miles to the south. He calculated their speed to be around 1,660 mph which was about three times that of any jet flying in the 1940s. His lowest estimate of their speed was 1,350 mph, also far faster than any aircraft.

The COMING of the SAUCERS

By Kenneth Arnold & Ray Palmer

Right: United States Marine Corps sighting, 1956. Flying over the Atlantic at night at 19,000 feet, Commander George Benson saw a cluster of lights below his aircraft. On board were 30 pilots, navigators and flight engineers. One of the lights broke away and headed for them, becoming a large, round object before "morphing" into a saucer shape. It was seen by several crewmen and took evasive action, tilting and slowing sharply before passing their port wing and flying with them, just 100 yards away. The shape of a dish inverted on top of another, and 400 feet in diameter, the object glowed around the rim and was sighted on ground radar. The object pulled ahead, tilted slightly and shot off at more than 2,500 mph. Precisely 30 years later, a larger UFO of very similar shape would make global news when it approached a Boeing 747.

9

CRASHES & CLOSE ENCOUNTERS
a sky full of strangeness

In July 1947 something fell from the sky on to desert ranchland in New Mexico. Men from the Roswell Army Air Field recovered the debris and issued a press release saying that this was a crashed flying saucer. Coming so soon after Kenneth Arnold's sighting it caused worldwide press interest. The U.S. military, however, quickly recanted and maintained the wreckage was merely that of a weather balloon.

People have since come forward who claim to have seen a crashed disk and small alien bodies at the time. Controversy still rages as to whether they are telling the truth or whether the crash debris was that of a secret Project Mogul balloon, as the U.S. military now claims.

In a less tangled tale, Father William Gill observed a craft and occupants at Boianai mission station in Papua New Guinea in 1959 on three successive nights. On June 26th Gill and 40 other people saw a bright white disk closely approach the mission building. The disk appeared to have an upper deck on which four figures were observed. These human-like beings seemed engaged in some task and would go in and out on the deck. At intervals a beam shone upward as the craft hovered perhaps 700 feet away. The object remained visible for four hours before being obscured by clouds.

Above: Artist's impression of the Roswell incident. Compounding the story, classified documents known as the MJ-12 papers began to circulate in 1984. These purported to show that the U.S. government had set up a committee of 12 senior officers and scientists in 1947 to examine recovered alien bodies and craft and report on the problem of ET visitation. Most researchers now believe that these papers were forged.

Above: Sketch by Rev. Norman Cruttwell. On the 2nd evening the UFO reappeared for 90 minutes with two smaller objects, sparkling brightly, and seeming closer than before. Again figures were seen working on deck. Gill and others waved and the ufonauts waved back. They waved both arms and the figures waved back with both arms. Gill also used a torch to flash signals at the UFO which appeared to respond. Eight UFOs were seen the next evening. Reports prepared by Father Gill were signed by 25 witnesses.

FRAUDS AND FAKERS
one born every day

Starting in the 1950s a number of people claimed to have had contact with the occupants of flying saucers from other worlds. Best known was George Adamski who lived in California and who said that he met with a Venusian from a landed cigar-shaped UFO in the desert. Some friends of Adamski watched from a distance and testified his claims were true. He produced photographs of flying saucers supposedly taken above his home near Mount Palomar. In 1953 he co-authored the book *Flying Saucers Have Landed* with Desmond Leslie and later wrote *Inside the Spaceships* describing his alleged journeys around the moon and to the planet Venus. During these trips with the "space brothers" he claimed to have seen cities, lakes, snowy mountains and forests on the far side of the moon.

Later U.S. and Russian photos of the moon from space probes put paid to any lingering doubts that Adamski's claims were other than fantasy. In the same way that Adamski founded a cult of believers in his extraterrestrial contacts, a Swiss farmer, Billy Meier, developed a cult following based on his alleged contacts with "beamships" from the Pleiades. During the 1970s Meier claimed that he flew in space with a Pleiadian lady named Semjase and also faked dozens of photos of beamship UFOs using models. Despite his being discredited there are still those who believe his claims.

Frauds and fakers have continued plying their trade up to the modern day. They are not, however, the subject of this book.

The five types of hubcap-style spacecraft in Billy Meier's photographs:

Meier claimed the Pleiadian female Semjase told him that the flying saucers cross interstellar space using a device which transports ship and crew in a twinkling of an eye over light-years.

Craft are crewed by up to seven cosmonauts, although the usual number is three.

A secondary propulsion system is used for slower travel near planets. This also creates artificial gravity.

Meier quotes Semjase as saying: "Our spaceships are projected by a screen of energy which automatically rejects any kind of resistance and every bit of matter."

Pleiadian spacecraft, claimed Meier, are constantly redeveloped and improved. Early types were superseded after centuries of usage because of radiation leakage problems.

EGG-SHAPED OBJECTS
Zamora craft and the Valensole incident

Police officer Lonnie Zamora was on routine patrol on April 24th, 1964 when he was called to investigate an explosion in Socorro, New Mexico. Driving out of town he saw in the near distance what he thought was an upturned car. It was in fact an egg-shaped object on "girder-like legs," complete with two entities, described by Zamora as children or small adults who seemed startled and surprised at his approach. When he got closer, the object rose with a loud roar, then a whirring noise and a blue flame or beam. Silently and with less flame, it moved away parallel to the ground, increasing speed as it did so. Zamora called for help on his radio and was joined by Sergeant Sam Chavez. They explored the site and found four angled impressions in the sandy soil where the "legs" had been, a part-burned bush and several small footprints and other impressions.

Another case from the same period reveals striking similarities. In a field of lavender plants in France on July 1st, 1965, Maurice Masse was working outside at about 5:45 a.m. when he heard a noise. Looking around, he saw an egg-shaped craft with a small dome on top, resting on six legs. Through a doorway set into the craft he could see two back-to-back seats. Outside were two small figures dressed in green, apparently investigating his lavender plants. One figure pointed a "rod" at the farmer. He found himself unable to move, but took note of their appearance: large heads, large eyes, thin mouths and pointed chins. They returned to the UFO and flew off, leaving him to suffer from extreme tiredness for months afterwards.

Above: The Zamora incident. Hector Quintanilla, Jr., former head of the U.S. Air Force Project Blue Book UFO research program, said: "This is the best-documented case on record, and still we have been unable, in spite of thorough investigation, to find the vehicle or other stimulus that scared Zamora to the point of panic."

Above: Maurice Masse's close encounter showing the "little men" who he discovered picking lavender on his farm in Valensole, France, on 1st July 1965. Masse was paralyzed by a "rod", not uncommon amongst UFO stories, and very similar to the magic wand of early fairy tales, which could paralyze humans.

Left: Elliptical or ellipsoidal UFOs are variously described as oval, rugby football, dirigible, egg, acorn or teardrop shaped. Sightings include the two above and those seen at the Isle of Väddö, Sweden, in 1956, Puerto Maldonado, Peru, in 1952, and Gerena, Spain, in 1978, to name but a few.

ABDUCTIONS
and intimate encounters

In 1975 a seven-man logging crew in Sitgreaves National Forest in Arizona stopped their truck to watch a glowing domed flying saucer. One of them, Travis Walton, jumped out and walked towards it. The object began to rumble and spin. Walton took cover but a beam of light knocked him to the ground. The others, terrified, sped away. Later they returned to look for Walton but found nothing.

The crew went to the local sheriff but searches revealed no sign of Walton and there was suspicion of foul play. All six woodcutters underwent polygraph tests and passed. Then, after five days' absence, a weak and confused Walton phoned his sister's house asking to be collected from Heber, twelve miles from where he had disappeared. His extraordinary story is told on the facing page (*opposite top*).

In an earlier case, Brazilian farmer Antonio Villas Boas was taken aboard a landed UFO in October 1957, where he willingly participated in sexual intercourse with a female humanoid (*center opposite*). Afterwards she rubbed her belly and pointed upward, which he took to mean that she was going to raise their child in space. The experience left a lasting impression on both the young man and the UFO fraternity and was a forerunner of abduction experiences worldwide.

Numerous studies have shown that experiences of abduction and sexual experimentation by aliens are far more common than many people realize. More and more individuals are reporting events ranging from the terrifying to the pleasurable. But are these real events or fantasies, and is there any historical precedent for such bizarre claims? The truth may be stranger than fiction, as we shall shortly see.

Left: Travis said that when he regained consciousness, he was lying in a room with three entities watching him. They were small with large bald heads. He tried unsuccessfully to attack them. He then entered a round room where a helmeted human stood. He led Walton to where several disk-shaped craft were parked and he saw other humans. An oxygen mask was placed over his face and he passed out. His next memory was lying in the road near Heber. More than 30 years later there is still controversy over the incidents despite Walton also having passed a polygraph test.

Above: Antonio Villas Boas was 23 when he saw an egg-shaped craft one night while plowing. His engine and headlights died and he was dragged to the craft by four short humanoids. Inside, he was stripped and covered in gel, then blood was taken from his chin and he was gassed and led into a room where a female humanoid with blue catlike eyes proceeded to mate with him.

Right: An estimated one million Americans believe they have had physical examinations by aliens. Sometimes frightening, for other people these memories can be elevating or beautiful. Harvard Professor John Mack described such beliefs as far too deep and widespread to ignore.

AWAY WITH THE FAERIES
getting closer to the truth

Alien abduction experiences are very often recalled under hypnosis. In Harvard Professor John Mack's later writings he stated that their consistency and frequency suggest that they are for real, but only in some strange way. Veronica Goodchild, a Jungian psychotherapist based at Pacifica Graduate Institute writes: "Some encounters seem to be taking place in a realm that is not clearly recognizable as either outside of ordinary reality or within one's interior world."

According to Mack, abductions belong to a special family of weird experiences. He argued that "... other cultures have always known that there were other realities, other beings, other dimensions. There is a world of other dimensions, of other realities that can cross over into our world." The West today, he said, was simply too materialistic to acknowledge or study these areas. Mack's ideas chime with ancient global beliefs in a faery realm, including numerous tales of humans who have been abducted by "the little people." Similarities between faery and alien tales abound even in the smallest details (*see opposite*).

Above and left: Could aliens and faeries be the same thing? Faeries wave a magic wand in order to paralyze or gain control over humans, and small aliens are reported to have pointed rod-like objects at observers to gain the same advantage. Both species can be described as often wearing green or gray all-in-one tunics. Both find humans sexy. The incubus (left) is a male demon that seduces and has its way with female humans. The succubus is a big-breasted female demon who extracts the life force from human men. Medieval scholars attributed sexual interactions like these to dreams, yet we now know that to those who experience them they are very real indeed. In fact, in dream-defying fashion, sexual intercourse between a woman and an incubus has apparently resulted, in some instances, in children. Hybrid children may be an anathema to many people, but they are well chronicled in faery and other literature, ancient and modern.

THE "WARMINSTER THING"
strange lights in the sky and men in black

There were well-documented and very curious goings-on around the town of Warminster, England, in the 1960s. Residents heard odd noises in the night and saw strange lights in the sky. Public meetings were called and people flocked to the area to see what newspapers dubbed the "Warminster Thing."

Local journalist Arthur Shuttlewood, after regular sky-watches on nearby hills at night, said he sensed the presence of large, invisible beings on the hills. He reported that unidentified lights in the sky responded to torches flashed on and off, by blinking themselves. Shuttlewood believed that these lights were extraterrestrial craft and the invisible beings their occupants. The Wiltshireman claimed that an ET, Karne, from the planet Aenstria, visited his home and gave him dire warnings about the world's future.

Meanwhile, 1950s and 60s UFO sightings became entangled with "Men in Black" (MIBs) who visited witnesses in their homes, mostly in the United States, demanding to see any UFO photographs, sometimes confiscating them. These black-suited men, often with wraparound sunglasses, would claim they were government agents or military officials investigating the UFO encounter. When witnesses tried later to contact them they would be met with official denial of any government interest or such personnel. Some researchers believed MIBs were aliens in disguise, while others thought they were indeed government officials checking out genuine UFO cases, but using aspects of theater to scare the contactees and add to the mystery.

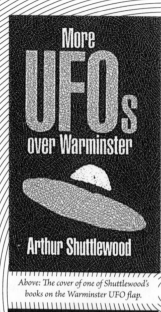

Above: The cover of one of Shuttlewood's books on the Warminster UFO flap.

Above: Artist's impression of the "Men in Black" from the popular 1970s Unexplained magazine.

Above and left: Two photos of the "Warminster Thing" taken in August 1965 by Gordon Faulkner showing distinctly different craft. The one on the left was taken at night, while the one above was shot in daytime from the center of Warminster town.

THE UMMO AFFAIR
and a strange landing in Russia

The UMMO affair began in 1966 with sightings near Madrid by witnesses who saw a flying saucer with the symbol Ж. Photographs and documents were supplied to the press and researchers by unknown UMMO sources. Life on the planet "UMMO," its government, technology, philosophy and other topics were described in detail.

Then, in 1989, from a pinkish glow, a UFO landed in a park in Voronezh, Russia, a city of 800,000. From it emerged three aliens and a robot. Boys playing football had witnessed its arrival and a crowd quickly gathered, peering into a hatch that had opened. Inside they saw a ten-foot-tall alien clad in silvery overalls and bronze boots. Two aliens (with Ж on their suits) and the robot then exited the vehicle. A boy screamed with fear but was paralyzed when one of the aliens looked at him. Others screamed as the UFO and creatures vanished before reappearing five minutes later. An alien pointed a 20-inch "gun" at a boy making him disappear. The aliens and robot then re-entered the craft and took off, at which point the boy reappeared.

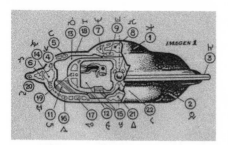

Above: Diagram of an UMMO craft received in the post.

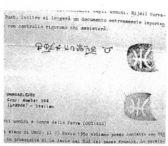

Above: One of the UMMO documents.

Above: UMMO craft appeared in cartoons of the time.

Above: Witness drawing of the Voronezh landing.

Above: More witness drawings of the Voronezh landing.

Above: Artist's impression of the Voronezh pinheads.

ACTION OVER IRAN
strange lights and malfunctioning systems

In September 1976 strange objects in the sky were seen by people living in Tehran, Iran. A fighter aircraft was sent to take a closer look but the pilot soon experienced communication and instrumentation problems and headed back to base. A second fighter plane approached the UFO and got a radar echo. The UFO was so bright the pilot was dazzled but as he got closer the object moved off at high speed.

The pilot, however, managed to keep pace with the UFO, which strobed with colored lights and discharged a smaller UFO that headed for the fighter plane. Fearing for his life, the pilot locked on to this possible threat with his missile system and prepared to fire. The missile system would not work. The pilot tried to avoid a collision by diving; the smaller UFO dived with him. When it returned to the main UFO, the missile system behaved normally again. The pilot was safe, but to this day the case—one of the best documented on record—remains a mystery.

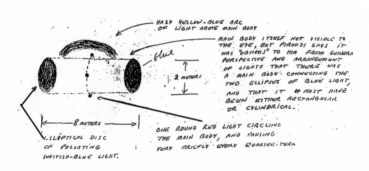

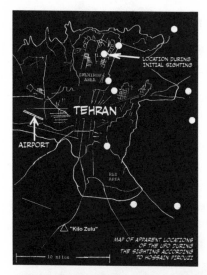

MAP OF APPARENT LOCATIONS
OF THE UFO DURING
THE SIGHTING ACCORDING
TO HOSSAIN PIROUZI

Above and facing page: Sketches of the 1976
Tehran UFO according to the pilots who saw it.
A similar UFO incident had occurred over the
American city of Los Angeles in 1942.

Above: A rare photograph of one of the UFOs over Los Angeles in 1942 during "The Battle of Los Angeles."
Initially the target was thought to be an attacking force from Japan but this image clearly shows a craft.

RENDLESHAM FOREST
U.S.AF servicemen witness a mysterious landing

An extraordinary series of UFO sightings and a reported landing occurred in Suffolk over three nights in late December 1980 in the woods just outside RAF Bentwaters, a major NATO airbase then controlled by the U.S. Air Force. Following reports of a bright UFO descending into the woods near the base, a patrol was sent out to investigate a suspected crashed aircraft. Witnesses saw a conical metallic craft hovering in a clearing. Staff Sgt. James Penniston said he approached a landed craft of unknown origin and touched it. Others saw red and yellow lights blinking among the trees.

The deputy base commander, Lt. Col. Charles Halt, entered the woods two nights later to investigate another incursion. He made a tape recording at the time and later wrote a memo to the UK Ministry of Defence. Some of the witnesses later said they were debriefed and made to sign statements denying they saw anything.

DEPARTMENT OF THE AIR FORCE
HEADQUARTERS 81ST COMBAT SUPPORT GROUP (USAFE)
APO NEW YORK 09755

13 Jan 81

REPLY TO
ATTN OF: CD

SUBJECT: Unexplained Lights

TO: RAF/CC

1. Early in the morning of 27 Dec 80 (approximately 0300L), two USAF security police patrolmen saw unusual lights outside the back gate at RAF Woodbridge. Thinking an aircraft might have crashed or been forced down, they called for permission to go outside the gate to investigate. The on-duty flight chief responded and allowed three patrolmen to proceed on foot. The individuals reported seeing a strange glowing object in the forest. The object was described as being metallic in appearance and triangular in shape, approximately two to three meters across the base and approximately two meters high. It illuminated the entire forest with a white light. The object itself had a pulsing red light on top and a bank(s) of blue lights underneath. The object was hovering or on legs. As the patrolmen approached the object, it maneuvered through the trees and disappeared. At this time the animals on a nearby farm went into a frenzy. The object was briefly sighted approximately an hour later near the back gate.

2. The next day, three depressions 1 1/2" deep and 7" in diameter were found where the object had been sighted on the ground. The following night (29 Dec 80) the area was checked for radiation. Beta/gamma readings of 0.1 milliroentgens were recorded with peak readings in the three depressions and near the center of the triangle formed by the depressions. A nearby tree had moderate (.05-.07) readings on the side of the tree toward the depressions.

3. Later in the night a red sun-like light was seen through the trees. It moved about and pulsed. At one point it appeared to throw off glowing particles and then broke into five separate white objects and then disappeared. Immediately thereafter, three star-like objects were noticed in the sky, two objects to the north and one to the south, all of which were about 10° off the horizon. The objects moved rapidly in sharp angular movements and displayed red, green and blue lights. The objects to the north appeared to be elliptical through an 8-12 power lens. The objects turned to full circles. The objects to the south was visible for two or three hours and beamed down a stream of light from time to time. Numerous individuals, including the undersigned, witnessed the activities in paragraphs 2 and 3.

CHARLES I. HALT, Lt Col, USAF
Deputy Base Commander

Above: Headline from News of the World. Left: The official letter confirming the incident. Below: Rendlesham Forest UFO symbols and sketches drawn by the airman who also said that the UFO was warm, as smooth as glass and changed colors.

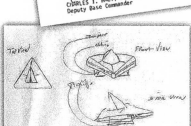

GREEN AND FISHY
two sightings of central shafts

Shortly after midnight on August 12th, 1983, 77-year-old Alfred Burtoo stopped fishing by a canal in Aldershot, England, to make a cup of tea. The sky was clear and Burtoo, a World War II veteran, observed a bright light descend nearby. His dog growled as two small human-like beings approached. Four feet tall and dressed in pale green overalls, "they had helmets of the same color with a visor that was blacked out." One of them beckoned to him and they walked to a craft on the towpath and entered it.

Inside, a central shaft stretched from floor to ceiling. There were no nuts or bolts visible and two other entities were present. Burtoo was asked to stand under a pale orange light and was told "You can go, you are too old and infirm for our purpose." Afterwards he heard a whining sound from the craft, which then flew away, lighting up the area with an intense light.

Another case involving a central shaft occurred on 17th June 1950 near Hasselbach, East Germany. Oscar Linke, a former mayor, and his daughter, Gabrielle, saw a large pan- or saucer-shaped, object, at dusk. From a distance of 40 yards they saw two "men" dressed in shiny metallic clothing looking at something on the ground. Walking to within 10 yards, Oscar noticed a "black conical tower" on top of the UFO. When Gabrielle called to him, the two entities jumped into the tower and the sides of the object glittered, turning from green to red. Rotating, the object rose slowly, while the tower, or shaft, slid down into the object and reappeared at its base.

Above: Artist's impression of the incident Alfred Burtoo encountered on 12th August 1983 whilst fishing by the canal in Aldershot. Burtoo clearly noticed a central shaft inside the craft, a feature of other UFO sightings.

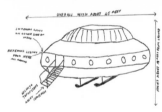

Left: Alfred Burtoo's own sketch of the extraordinary craft he saw that day. After the craft took off Burtoo calmly finished his cup of tea.

Right: Artist's impression of the UFO seen on 17th June 1950 by Oscar Linke and his daughter Gabrielle near Hasselbach, East Germany. The object was seen by many local people as it flew away as a bright light. Investigating the "landing" site, Oscar found a circular depression corresponding to the width of the shaft. The ground there was disturbed, presumably, he thought, by the shaft as it dropped through the object. The same sort of shaft was described by Alfred Burtoo in his sighting.

THE HUDSON VALLEY WAVE
vast triangular craft in night sky

Between 1983 and 1986 hundreds, possibly thousands, of people saw huge triangular UFOs in the night skies of upstate New York and Connecticut. They moved slowly and silently across the sky, often just a few hundred feet up, and were frequently described as being "as large as a football field." One astonished witness, Ed Burns, said "If there is such a thing as a flying city, this was a flying city. It was not a small craft. It was huge!" Many witnesses believed they were seeing spaceships from beyond Earth. No sound was generally heard and they displayed bright red, blue, green or white lights seemingly embedded in their dark fuselage. The light configuration would often change, with lights going out and others coming on. Circular UFOs also were seen (*see Randy Etting's 1987 Connecticut photograph, below left*). Sometimes all the lights would go off rendering the UFO invisible. Some witnesses saw these craft from close quarters, hovering over lakes or, in one case, over a nuclear power plant at Buchanan, N.Y. (*opposite top*). These were emphatically not U.S. stealth aircraft. Boomerang-shaped UFOs had first appeared in the 1960s.

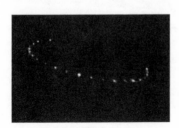

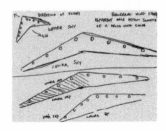

Above: The Indian Point Nuclear Reactor complex at Buchanan, New York. On July 24th, 1984, a UFO was witnessed by twelve police officers hovering between the tower and the dome for fifteen minutes.

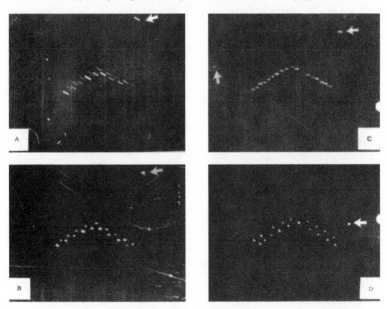

Above: Strange boomerang-shaped lights photographed during the 1951 Lubbock, Texas, UFO wave. Opposite. right: Illustration by Monique O'Driscoll of UFO seen on February 26th, 1983, Lake Carmel, N.Y.

UFOS OVER BELGIUM
unexplained flying triangles

Over Brussels, Liège, Namur and other towns in Belgium between 1988 and 1991 large numbers of people saw strange black triangular craft quite unlike any known plane.

In one incident two gendarmes in a patrol car, Heinrich Nicholl and Hubert Montigny, spotted one of the objects in the sky near Eupen on November 29 1989. They described it as the size of a football field floating in the air with powerful "headlights" shining down from its three corners. For an hour they followed it as it hovered or traveled silently over fields, sometimes bathing the ground below with light. Shortly afterwards two other gendarmes saw another similar UFO in the sky over La Calamine, eight miles north of the city. It hovered low over a church and they saw a pulsating red light descend from the triangle's center and fly around before returning. Then the three white corner lights moved together and merged into one single light which flew off, leaving the sky empty.

At a press conference called by the Belgian Air Force, Major General Wilfried de Brouwer described how on several occasions F-16 jets had pursued such UFOs. Despite radar lock-on, the mystery craft had flown away at high speed outperforming the interceptors. He said openly there was something going on over Belgium that was "beyond our control." The USAF confirmed to him that none of its aircraft or experimental planes were over Belgium at that time. Major de Brouwer failed to identify the origin and intentions of the craft but maintained that something was regularly infringing NATO air space.

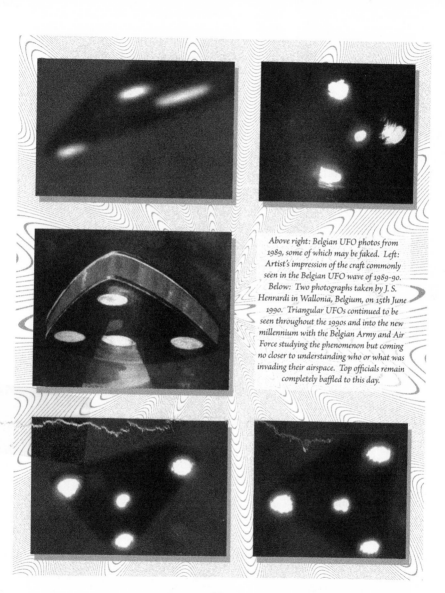

Above right: Belgian UFO photos from 1989, some of which may be faked. Left: Artist's impression of the craft commonly seen in the Belgian UFO wave of 1989-90. Below: Two photographs taken by J. S. Henrardi in Wallonia, Belgium, on 15th June 1990. Triangular UFOs continued to be seen throughout the 1990s and into the new millennium with the Belgian Army and Air Force studying the phenomenon but coming no closer to understanding who or what was invading their airspace. Top officials remain completely baffled to this day.

A MULTIPLE WITNESS EVENT
a classic "bend in the road" case

A remote and sparsely populated country, Australia is testament to Dr. Allen Hynek's assertion that some of the best UFO cases occur where human beings are few and far between, and surprisingly often occur in a bend in the road, at night.

On the evening of August 8th, 1993, Kelly Cahill was in her car near Melbourne with her husband and three children when she saw an orange-glowing circular object on the ground and with round windows around it, ablazing. Later that night, on their way home, Kelly saw a second UFO, close to the site of her earlier sighting. This time her husband saw it too, before it zoomed off. Then, as they drove on, a large bright light appeared in the middle of the road—another classic attribute of UFO behavior, according to Hynek. And then the UFO, or light, suddenly "switched off."

Later the couple realized they were missing an hour or two of time, and Kelly noticed a strange triangular mark on her navel. Months later Kelly began to remember that during the "missing time" she and her husband had got out of the car and met with a group of 7-foot-tall black aliens with glowing red eyes. It also turned out that Kelly's original sighting had also been experienced by three occupants of another car—people who neither she nor her husband knew.

This multiple witness account, with its missing time, and psychic behavior experienced by both sets of witnesses, has turned the case into a UFO cause célèbre, especially as there was a witness in a third car. Kelly Cahill can be seen describing the case on *youtube.com*.

Left: A classic illustrated example of a "Bend in the Road" UFO case. A significant number of UFO cases occur in remote locations at a bend in the road at night.

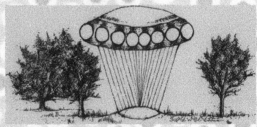

Right: Artist's impression of the craft witnessed by Kelly Cahill on two occasions on August 8th, 1993.

Left: Artist's impression of the tall black aliens who Kelly Cahill later remembered meeting during her initial period of "missing time."

SEEING THINGS
auras and orbs

In recent years one of the most widespread unidentified aerial phenomena has been the mass recording of "orbs" of light on digital cameras. Typically these balls of light appear on digital camera pictures taken at night with a flash. Some people say they can manifest a room full of orbs just by meditation. Sceptics have claimed that the orbs are nothing more than the reflection of dust particles or moisture in the air, but this does not explain how someone sitting motionless in a room can bring about photographable changes.

It has even been claimed by some people that orbs could be living beings, faeries (*see page 18*), or even spirits of the dead. About 1 in 25 people say they occasionally see orbs or flashes of light with their own eyes in broad daylight. This is similar to the proportion of people who regularly see "auras" of some kind around living things, possibly an electromagnetic effect. Could orbs be timely clues to mysterious realms of reality which mankind has forgotten exist?

Snap some orb pictures at home and see what you think!

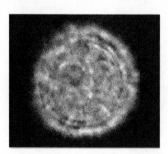 

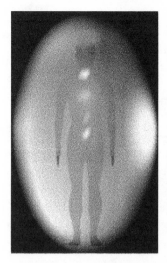

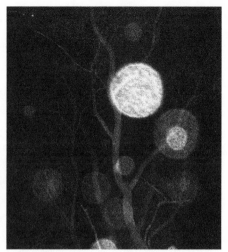

Above: Artist's impression of a human "aura" and "chakras" as seen by 1 in 25 people. In the same way that 1 in 10 people are synesthetic, others can "see" electromagnetic fields.

Above, below and left. Photographs of "orbs" taken on a digital camera by Cedar Rivers in Australia. Orbs seem to respond to meditation, congregating around certain places. Visit Cedar's Web page www.celticgardens.com.au for more images.

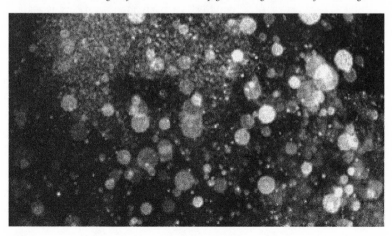

WORKING WITH UFOS
close encounters of the fifth kind

In 1972, in his book *The UFO Experience: A Scientific Inquiry*, astronomer and UFO researcher J. Allen Hynek classified three kinds of encounters with UFOs, a list which was later expanded to five.

A close encounter of the *first* kind involves seeing flying saucers, odd lights or unknown aerial phenomena. A close encounter of the *second* kind requires physical effects, heat or radiation, ground markings, paralysis or missing time effects. Close encounters of the *third* kind involve the sighting of "animate beings." In close encounters of the *fourth* kind, the surroundings of the observer are transformed, e.g., visiting spaceships or journeying to fairyland. Finally, close encounters of the *fifth* kind are bilateral contact events produced through telepathy, meditation and conscious group activity.

This last category of encounter has been increasing significantly in recent years with more and more groups and individuals claiming to be able to "invite" UFOs to appear. For example, Steven Greer's pioneering CSETI groups are composed of strong visualizers and meditators. They go to UFO dense areas and claim to work with the entities, asking where and when they should wait. Lights and craft are apparently filmed, and alien beings communicated with. Large craft sometimes exchange flashes of light with the team before flying off to be seen by hundreds of witnesses, on rare occasions leaving crop markings below where they first appeared.

As more and more people become interested in the reality of UFOs we can only expect more of this kind of thing.

Above: Groups of meditators and telepaths claim to be able to contact UFOs and their occupants, receiving instructions of where and when to wait for craft to appear. Telepathy seems to be the language.

Above: Devil's Tower, Wyoming, the center of the landing in Spielberg's Close Encounters of the Third Kind. In many ways the film really described a close encounter of the fifth kind for the protagonist.

Exploring the UFO Reality
fact may be stranger than fiction

Researching the UFO phenomenon can be extremely difficult. Not only do we not know where and when to find them, but many of the more interesting events, affecting national security as they do, tend to be covered up, or "shown" to be hoaxes. Government attempts to find out what is really going on, such as the United States Air Force study Project Blue Book [1952-1970], which collected and analyzed thousands of UFO reports, are largely kept secret from the public despite their inconclusive findings. Add to this the fact that it is useful to the military to have a general public which tends to think things they don't recognize might be alien spacecraft and you have a thick soup. Nevertheless, thousands and thousands of people have seen strange things, and they are not all stupid or crazy.

A consistent feature of UFO sightings is their eerie "otherness." Arthur C. Clarke wrote that "any sufficiently advanced alien technology is indistinguishable from magic," and it has been suggested that UFOs may be using other dimensions beyond our three, or that we might actually be detecting alien messages or possibly seeing non-physical aliens. In fact we may be living in the midst of alien realities, largely unaware of them, or even in virtual realities created by aliens.

Local UFO sightings still stir up interest

By Susan L. Wood
RCN Staff

EXETER — A series of une-

by John Fuller.

Fuller, who was scheduled to appear, was absent because of medical problems.

UFO sighted in village

A UFO was spotted hovering over a West Halifax field where corn circles have appeared in the...

Above: News cuttings from the archives of Flying Saucer Review. Ordinary people see extraordinary things they cannot explain. Local newspapers often take a much more open-minded approach than the mainstream media.

VISITORS FROM INNER SPACE
age-old archetypal visions

Could UFOs be archetypal visions, modern versions of apparitions of St. Michael or the Virgin Mary? In his book *Flying Saucers*, the great psychologist Carl Jung [1875-1961] argued that external events mirror internal psychic states and that the archetypes, previously seen as gods, angels or fairies, appear today as UFOs in response to the collective human psyche, obsessed by fast-changing new technologies.

Jung's theory was echoed in *The Flying Saucer Vision* by John Michell [1933-2009], who speculated that UFOs emanated from the human psyche. UFOs, he wrote, are "portents of a radical change in human consciousness coinciding with the dawn of the Aquarian Age."

Senior British intelligence officer and diplomat Gordon Creighton [1908-2003] considered UFOs to be djinns—naughty spirits parading as physical craft. Ralph Noyes [1914-1998], a high-ranking British Ministry of Defence and Royal Air Force officer, specialising in unexplained aerial sightings, said of UFOs, "We really don't know what they are. They play with us, with our pilots and soldiers; they seem to have a sense of humor."

Contemporary thinker and writer Patrick Harpur holds that the human psyche extends beyond traditionally accepted confines of the human body as an integral part of a greater reality. Reality is not at all what we think it is. UFOs, he maintains, bear all the hallmarks of a Mercurial communication, timely confusions brought to us by the trickster messenger of the gods. It is our erroneous over-fixation and certainty about the physical nature of reality which has naturally prompted an appropriate reply from the other side of the mirror.

Above: The Fairy Raid by Sir Joseph Noel Paton. Today we observe the same time-honored and global phenomenon of lights, missing-time and encounters with "elves"–but as UFOs and alien abductions.

Above: Apparitions suit their time and place. Some of the many photographs of the apparition of the Virgin Mary which appeared at Zeitoun Church in Egypt from 1968-71, witnessed by thousands of people.

So What Are ETs?

whatever you want them to be

Charles Fort, born in 1874 and often described as the first "ufologist," collected reports of unusual phenomena and concluded UFOs were alien visitations. Many thinkers since have tended to agree with him.

But are they benign? Some UFO watchers believe that the extra-terrestrial craft contain aliens who regularly kidnap humans to keep as slaves, using our blood for food or other purposes, and our genes for creating a hybrid species. They point to the weird and widespread occurrence of cattle and other animal mutilations across the world, where animals are often found completely drained of their blood, dumped as from a height in an area with no tracks leading to it, and with surgical-type wounds like the precise removal of flesh from a jawbone along with linear cuts and cauterized edges. The subject has been the study of two independent federal investigations in the U.S.

UFO cults are increasing. In the early 20th century, Welsh Christian Mary Jones and her fellow Revivalists preached that moving balls of light were proof that God was trying to communicate with them (strange blue lights had been seen in the area since 1877). In the early 20th century the spiritual order Subud was founded by Bapak Subuh in Indonesia after seeing a ball of light in the sky. Modern American cults such as Heaven's Gate and more recently the Raëlians both have the doctrinal reality of evolved psychic ETs at their core.

The UFO phenomenon therefore spans all points of view, from sinister paranoid outlooks ("we are being farmed"), to evolutionary spiritual models of the universe ("they are waiting for us to awake").

Above: Artists' impressions of spaceships look nothing like the simple UFOs people actually report seeing. Could this be evidence that ET technology is in some way postphysical, postmaterialistic, as cultists claim?

Left: Are aliens evolved beings coming to bring us enlightenment, or are they farming us for reasons as yet unclear? Could the truth lie somewhere in between? Perhaps, in the same way that biologists travel in small numbers to study the Amazonian rainforest, it tends to be the smaller ET research vessels that we encounter here on this still relatively primitive and materialistic planet of unevolved ecotrashers.

THE FERMI PARADOX
and the Drake equation

So is the universe teeming with life or not? An equation first devised by Frank Drake at the University of California suggests that it probably is. This, however, begs the question, first expressed by Enrico Fermi of the Los Alamos Laboratory ... "so where are they all?"

It turns out that for biological life you need to be the right distance from the right star, and the right distance from the galactic center (to have the right mix of elements). You also seriously need to *not* have a supernova go off nearby sending you back to the slime age.

Electricity was only discovered 150 years ago! What technology might be around in a few million years time? And what do intelligent mobile physical beings like us eventually evolve into anyway (assuming they don't pollute themselves to death first)? So ... UFOs?

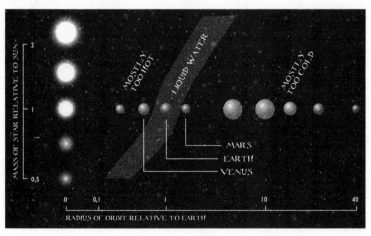

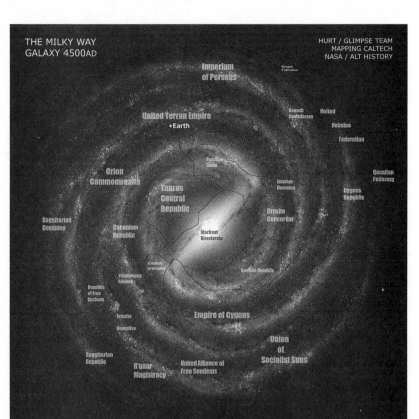

Above: An imaginative future mapping of our own Milky Way galaxy of 100 billion stars. Why haven't aliens landed on the White House lawn? Or have they in fact? Why do UFOs so often appear to ordinary people going about their business? Why do they so often appear near military and aviation subjects? Is Earth in quarantine of some kind? Are we too primitive to bother with? Are we looking for the wrong signal - the SETI Institute scanned for analog signals in yesterday's analog age and today it looks for white noise digital signals in the digital age. What's the next communication age? Could the end game for evolved biotechnology be not physical at all but psychic or entangled in some way? These are all answers to the Fermi Paradox. The picture assumes that intelligent life carries on evolving along physical territorial lines, but the majority of UFO evidence points towards something much stranger.

LIFE ELSEWHERE
variation and convergence

Life on Earth needs water. However, on cold moons and planets it is possible that liquid methane could act just as well as a carrier medium for life. Indeed, the diversity of moons and dynamic planets within our own solar system continues to astonish scientists, so life and alienkind could probably take on all sorts of forms and shapes. Or could they?

Marsupial (pouched) and placental mammals diverged from a single common ancestor over 100 million years ago before evolving along their two paths. So the marsupial mammals of Australia should be different from their placental cousins in the rest of the world. Instead, species that occupy similar niches are remarkably similar in design (*see below*). It turns out that if you want to see clearly, eat bugs, swim fast with big teeth, burrow in the dark or manipulate tools, there is a best design for doing that. Evolution finds these designs again and again.

This is called convergent evolution, and it suggests that aliens and alien plants could look very like their earthly counterparts. Even DNA seems optimized, so aliens might really be more like cousins.

Flying Squirrel — Marsupial Flying Phalanger — Wolf — Marsupial Tasmanian Wolf

Anteater — Marsupial Anteater — Ocelot — Marsupial Native Cat

Mole — Marsupial Mole — Ground Hog — Marsupial Wombat

Above: Life may exist not only on distant planets, but on their moons too. In our own solar system the moons Europa and Titan could both be suitable crucibles for biological life.

Above: Similar yet different. Life on other planets may not look too different from the successful forms we see on Earth. Convergent evolution suggests that some designs are just the best solution.

WHAT IS THE UNIVERSE?
why so weirdly life-friendly

In the 1970s two Cambridge professors, John Barrow and Frank Tipler, noticed a very strange thing about our universe—it seems to be *very* finely tuned to maximize the chances for biological life, so finely tuned in fact that if you fiddle with any of the constants of physics, even slightly, then the entire universe becomes totally inhospitable to the formation of complex structures of any kind.

This bizarre *Anthropic Principle*, as it is now known, suggests that the universe may be much stranger and more organic than we imagine. It could be that living, conscious, organic forms are the driving forces of the universe, rather than being by-products. To get round the problem some physicists have proposed a "multiverse" where our own life-filled universe is chance miracle amidst squillions of other lifeless ones, while other scientists have suggested that our universe could be the child of successful parent universes. Trendy *Matrix*-style theories hold that the universe seems perfect for life because it is in fact a computer simulation of some kind, a designed virtual reality.

The fact that the universe is electromagnetic and connected also suggests that it might be a huge mind (*see opposite*), possibly even like a "God." Could a vast prescient quantum consciousness have imagined its own perfect tuning, trying everything like a quantum computer and coming up with the best solution right from the start? What role then might locally entangled biological consciousnesses like us play?

Whatever they are, UFOs remind us of our origin and possible destiny in the stars, free of territorial squabbles and narrow definitions.

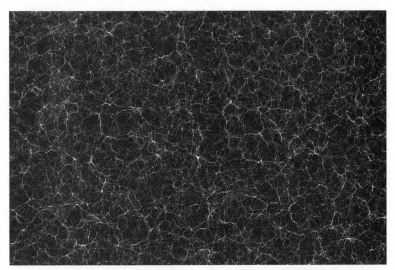

Above: A small part of the universe shown at a macro level, zoomed out a long way. At this scale the structure of space fizzes with electrical energy, with galaxy clusters strung along plasma filaments (see enlargement below).

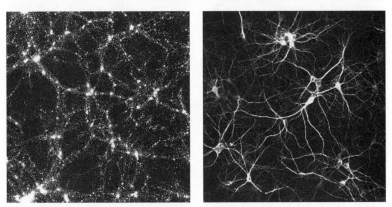

Above: The plasma filamentation of space connects galaxy clusters, stringing them along invisible electro-magnetic cables. On the left we see large galaxy clusters connected by filaments of smaller galaxy clusters. The structure is reminiscent of a neural network, shown right. Could the universe be a giant brain?

100 NOTABLE UFO SIGHTINGS

1878, January. John Martin, a farmer living 6 miles north of Dallas, Texas, was out hunting and saw a dark object in the sky. Its peculiar shape and speed of approach riveted his attention. It came directly overhead. He compared the object to a large saucer, the first recorded use of the term before 1947.

1909. Peterborough, England. At 5:10 a.m. in different parts of the city, two police officers reported a mystery airship with a long oblong body, a searchlight and "the steady buzz of a high power engine" as it passed overhead.

1910. Invercargill, New Zealand. Witnesses of a flying cigar included the vicar, the mayor and a policeman. On the object, a "man" stood by a "door," shouting in an unknown language. The door closed and the object accelerated away.

1914. Ontario, Canada. A UFO floating on the water of Georgian Bay was seen by eight observers. Human-like entities on the craft held a hose that dipped into the water. On seeing the witnesses all but one returned inside; the remaining entity was still outside when the craft took off.

1942, February. Los Angeles, California. A succession of UFO night alerts in southern California. Los Angeles was blacked out while searchlights converged on a UFO which was fired at by U.S. Army gunners. Claims that the UFO was a weather balloon were discounted as a balloon would have been shot down.

1944-45. During World War II many U.S. pilots flying over Germany and the Pacific reported seeing fast-moving glowing spherical objects flying close to their aircraft, often in formation with them. These fiery red, orange and white balls of light became known as "foo fighters." They appeared to toy with aircraft as if intelligently controlled but not threatening.

1944, August. France. En route back to England, a Lancaster bomber crew of eight saw a huge disk-shaped object emerge from a long row of lights, and observed it for three minutes before it disappeared in a flash of light in less than a second. When debriefed, the crew was told not to talk to anyone about the incident and not to record the sighting in their log books.

1948, October 1st. Fargo, North Dakota. In this well documented case, experienced pilot Lieutenant George F. Gorman had at least two near collisions – during a 27 minute encounter – with a UFO that made an "unbelievable" maneuver directly in front of his aircraft. Witnesses on the ground also saw the UFO.

1951. U.S. astronaut Deke Slayton saw a UFO when testing a P-51 Mustang fighter near Minneapolis, Minnesota, on a clear day. He saw what he thought was a kite, or a weather balloon at 10,000 feet. When he got closer he saw it was a small disk moving at his speed of 300 mph. Then it took off, accelerated, and vanished.

1952, July. A New York to Miami flight. Captain William B. Nash, one of two pilot witnesses of UFOs that night, said: "They flipped on edge, the sides to the left of us going up and the glowing surfaces facing right. Though the bottom surfaces did not become clearly visible, we had the impression that they were unlighted. The exposed edges, also unlighted, appeared to be about 15 feet thick, and the top surface, at least seemed flat. In shape and proportion, they were much like coins. Their shape was clearly outlined and evidently circular. The edges were well-defined, not phosphorescent or fuzzy in the least."

1952, August. Haneda. At an Air Force Base in Japan, an American fighter plane got a radar lock on a disk-shaped UFO. Major Dewey Fournet considered it a spaceship from another planet.

1952, October. In Oloron, France, civilians saw over 30 red spherical UFOs accompanying a cylindrical-shaped object. From them came a white, hair-like substance, since nicknamed "angel hair," which covered telephone wires, tree branches and house roofs.

1952, September. Air Force Topcliffe, England. A silver disk-shaped object followed an RAF Gloster Meteor aircraft, rotating while hovering. Over the North Sea, six other RAF aircraft followed a spherical object, which followed one of the aircraft back to base.

1954, June. Near Goose Bay, Labrador, an entire flight crew and passengers observed a large, shape-changing UFO, accompanied by six smaller objects, for 18 minutes. Captain James Howard said, "There is no question ... it was being intelligently handled."

1954, July. A U.S.AF F-94 Starfire crashed into Walesville, New York, killing several people, while pursuing a fast UFO.

1954, August. An "electric green ball" was seen descending vertically behind a hill in Tananarive, capital of Madagascar. It reappeared and then flew at about 350 feet up along the principal street in front of thousands of amazed inhabitants. Behind this flew a silvery metallic craft about 130 feet long with blue exhaust flames. All the city's lights failed, coming on again when the aerial procession departed. Dogs were running and howling and oxen panicked, breaking out of their enclosures.

1954, October. RAF North Weald UK. Flt. Lt. James Salandin, in a RAF Gloster Meteor F-8, narrowly missed two UFOs over Southend-on-Sea at 16,000 feet. The objects were circular – one silver colored, the other gold. Salandin almost collided.

1954, November. Rosa Lotti, a 40-year-old peasant woman, was walking to Cennina, Italy, when she saw a vertical "spindle" like two joined cones standing in the ground. From behind this craft came two little men, 3 feet tall, who approached her in a friendly way. They spoke a language sounding like Chinese. Then they snatched the flowers she was carrying and a stocking. She fled. A deep hole was later found at the site.

1954, December. At Floresta near Caracas, Venezuela, a doctor and his father were driving from La Carlota Airfield to Miranda Avenue. They saw two little men run into a thicket. Then a luminous disk rose from behind the thicket darting off into the sky at great speed. A sharp sizzling sound was heard.

1955, July. Thirty witnesses saw a saucer-shaped object hover above a street in Bexley, London, on a cloudless day. Car engines nearby stalled as the UFO made a humming noise and landed. A few streets away, another UFO landed.

1956, August. At Lakenheath-Bentwaters, England, UFOs were seen by U.S.AF radar, one flying at more than 4,000 mph, another over 12,000 mph. They were also seen visually by RAF pilots. The UFOs sometimes traveled in formation and converged to form a larger object that performed sharp turns.

1957, July. Over the U.S. a USAF B-47 bomber was followed for 700 miles by a bright light that was picked up by on-board ECM equipment. It performed very rapid turns almost instantly and without slowing down, before blinking out. Another bomber pilot, Lieutenant Colonel Bruce Bailey, later said there were other cases like this one and that he was present at one of them.

1957, November. At Fort Itaipu near São Paulo, Brazil, two sentries saw a brilliant light descend from the night sky and head at high speed towards the fort. It was circular, about 100 feet wide, and shone an intense orange. The men were frightened though armed with a submachine gun, yet didn't dare fire or raise the alarm. The UFO emitted a humming noise, and a wave of heat hit the men, setting their clothes on fire. One fell and fainted. The other took cover. Their screams alerted nearby troops, but the lights went out before they came. Minutes later, the lighting came back again and the heat wave stopped. Some soldiers saw the UFO going up into the sky.

1960, August. Two patrolmen in Red Bluff, California, thought an airliner was about to crash, before they saw it was a UFO that suddenly shot upward, performing complex aerial maneuvers.

1960, October. In Cressy, Tasmania, Australia, Rev. and Mrs. Lionel Browning saw a cigar-shaped "'mothership" and flying disks. The case was thoroughly investigated by various authorities.

1962, May-July. NASA pilot Joseph Walker filmed five or six UFOs, saying that one of his tasks was to detect UFOs during his X-15 flights. Major Robert White also reported a "grayish" UFO nearby, during one of his flights. NASA astronauts Gordon Cooper and Edgar Mitchell have both said UFOs are for real.

1963, November. Off the coast of Argentina, a huge, round, silent UFO appeared, pulling various ship's compasses, including that of a navy transport vessel, towards it.

1964, September. Cisco Grove, Placer County, California. A hunter hid up a tree while a UFO zigzagged nearby and stopped 50 yards away. "Aliens" tried to shake him out of the tree. Terrified, he fired arrows at them and remained under attack for much of the night, during which more "aliens" arrived. A fellow hunter also reported seeing a UFO.

1965, December. U.S. astronauts Frank Borman and James Lovell saw a UFO near them in orbit during their 14-day flight in *Gemini* 7. Borman reported a "bogey" some distance from their capsule. Cape Kennedy Mission Control suggested it was the final stage of their Titan booster rocket. Borman said that he could see that, but also something completely different.

1965. Exeter, New Hampshire, 1965. A series of UFO sightings and terrifying close encounters with fast-moving objects at night were witnessed by many respected members of the local community including deeply shocked police and military personnel.

1966, January. In Tully, Queensland, Australia, farmer George Pedley heard a loud hissing sound above the noise of his tractor and saw a large, gray, spinning saucer-shaped object, some 25 feet across and 9 feet high, rise from a swamp and fly off fast.

1966, April. In Portage County, Ohio, several police officers chased a UFO which flew along Route 224. Initially two officers saw a 40-foot UFO which flew about 75 feet over their car and shone down a beam of light. It emitted a loud humming sound. When it took off to the SE they followed. Other officers were alerted and joined the chase. Air Force jets were scrambled to intercept but the UFO vanished at high speed. Project Blue Book said the police were chasing the planet Venus, which the officers involved said was ridiculous.

1966, November. Near Point Pleasant, West Virginia, Mr. & Mrs. Roger Scarberry and another couple saw a 7-foot-tall creature shaped like a man but with wings 10 feet across. It had red glowing eyes and flew away into the night. Over a hundred people saw this creature on different occasions at the time and it was subsequently called "Mothman." John Keel relates how the town experienced a UFO flap, visits by "Men in Black" and claims of alien contact as well as other bizarre phenomena.

1967, February. Farmer Claude Edwards saw a gray-green mushroom-shaped object, 18 feet across, in a pasture near his Tuscumbia, Missouri, farm. Several small figures moved rapidly under the object. He approached but when just 15 feet away he was stopped by a "force field." The craft then rocked and rose silently into the air. Its central shaft retracted into the base and it flew away leaving a hole in the ground.

1967, May. Prospector Stefan Michalak near Falcon Lake in the wilds of Manitoba, Canada, saw two cigar-shaped objects descend from the sky, one of which landed near him. He approached the craft and heard voices. A door opened and he saw lights inside. He touched the craft and his gloves melted. It took off and a blast of hot gas knocked him to the ground setting his shirt on fire. He was treated for 2nd and 3rd degree burns.

1967, October. In Shag Harbour, Nova Scotia, a UFO with four bright lights flashing in sequence hovered over the water, tilted at a 45-degree angle and descended rapidly into the sea. It was joined by a 2nd UFO. Both left the sea days later and at least one was tracked on sonar. Witnesses included military personnel.

1967, October. A major UFO "flap" in Devon UK. The Royal Observatory declared, "There is something up there which is not a star or a planet." In one case a bright, pulsating, cross-shaped object, at tree-top height, was seen by two policemen from 40 yards at 4 a.m. They followed it for 15 minutes at 80 mph. At 4:23 a.m. it was joined by a second object. A motorist also saw it. The UFO disappeared around 5 a.m. after a 14-mile chase.

1967, November. Mr. and Mrs. Masgutov of Kazan, USSR, saw a reddish ringed object shaped like Saturn which hovered in the sky spinning for ten minutes. It was self-luminous, the flat ring of similar color and seemed to spin faster before disappearing.

1969, October. U.S. President Jimmy Carter had a sighting of an unidentified object in the sky over Leary, Georgia, together with 10-20 other witnesses. "It was a kind of green light that appeared in the western sky right after sundown. It got brighter and brighter. And then it eventually disappeared. It didn't have any solid substance to it. It was just a very peculiar-looking light. None of us could understand what it was."

1969, October. Crew members and commander of a Chilean Navy destroyer saw up to six UFOs, which were also picked up on radar. When one of the objects moved over the ship, the vessel's power went out. Chilean scientists had earlier declared, "There is scientific evidence that strange objects visit our planet."

1968, November. South East France. In the early hours a French physician saw two glowing objects after being wakened by his child, who was crying and pointing at the window. The doctor experienced physiological effects, including rejuvenating effects on physical injuries, and recurring skin marks on his body.

1971, November. Ron Johnson was tending the sheep on the family farm in Delphos, Kansas, when a mushroom-shaped UFO appeared in the night sky and landed nearby. Very bright and about 8 feet across, it made a loud vibrating noise. It ascended again but left behind a glowing ring on the ground. Traces of the ring remained visible for years.

1973, October. Coyne, Ohio. Four army helicopter crew got close to a gray, metallic-looking, cigar-shaped object, with unusual lights and maneuvers, flying between Columbus and Cleveland.

1974, September. Farmer Edwin Fuhr in Saskatchewan, Canada, saw five spinning metallic dome-shaped objects hovering just above the ground in a field of his. After a few minutes each of them silently ascended vertically leaving a smoky trail and flew away. They left behind flattened rings in the long grass, 8 to 11 feet across. Two days later a further such ring was found in the field.

1975, August. At Alamogordo, New Mexico, U.S.AF Staff Sergeant Charles L. Moody saw a glowing, metallic, disk-shaped object, as it approached him. The UFO rose and disappeared. He said he was taken on board by "aliens" and then released.

1975, October. Loring Air Force Base, Maine, U.S.A. Strange events at Loring AFB resulted in the conclusion that a UFO, the size of a car, was "demonstrating a clear intent in the weapons storage area." The base was put on full alert.

1976, January. Three women near Stanford, Kentucky, saw a bright red object in the sky, which one of them at first thought was an aircraft on fire. Bigger than two houses, it descended nearby and took control of their car before they were abducted.

1976, April. George Wheeler, a police officer of Elmwood, Wisconsin, drove to investigate an orange glow in the sky near Tuttle Hill. "My God, it's one of those UFOs again," he shouted over the police radio. "It's huge – bigger than a two-story house." Next a blue ray shot from the UFO hitting him and the squad car. The radio failed and the car was a wreck. Wheeler was knocked unconscious and never recovered, believing he had radiation poisoning. Hospitalized for weeks, he died six months later.

1976, June. An "alien sphere" and lights were seen by multiple witnesses in the Canary Islands. Two 8-10 foot tall "alien beings" with large helmeted heads were seen on the "platform," or "control center," of the transparent sphere.

1976, August. Four students in Maine's Allagash Wilderness encountered a huge oval, glowing object rising above trees and engulfing them in a beam of light. Later, under hypnosis, they described being abducted into the craft and physically examined.

1976, August. Near Jaboticatubas, Brazil, Cicilio Higinio Pereira was attacked by a UFO when walking home with two female neighbors. On a dirt road in an isolated area they all ran from a bright light that came towards them. Cicilio fell and the huge object like an open umbrella came down over him. He smelled sulfur in the air and saw through a door 2 or 3 small men inside the craft. Then it vanished. Very ill from what might have been radiation poisoning, he died of this sickness two months later.

1977, March. French Air Force pilot Hervé Giraud flying a Mirage IV at 32,000 feet at night encountered an extremely bright object on a collision course. He took evasive action and radioed military radar. The object had not registered on ground radar. It, or another object, then reappeared and once more Giraud had to bank sharply before returning safely to his base at Luxeuil.

1978? Russian Professor Vladimir Azhazha: "One day ... one of our icebreakers was working its way in the Arctic Ocean when a brilliant spherical craft suddenly broke through the ice and flew up vertically, showering the vessel with fragments of ice. All the sailors on deck and the officers on the bridge saw it. And it was hard to deny the hole in the ice." He rejected it as a missile firing.

1978, October. Bass Strait, Australia. Pilot Frederick Valentich radioed ground control that a large unidentified "aircraft" with a metallic-like sheen was orbiting above him. After 17 seconds of metallic sounds there was silence. Valentich is still missing.

1978, December. Guardsman Pier Fortunato Zanfretta was on midnight duty in Genoa, Italy, when he was "abducted" by "monsters about 10 feet tall, with hairy green skin, yellow triangular eyes and red veins across the forehead." The aliens used a "luminous device" to translate their words into Italian.

1978, December. New Zealand pilots saw a UFO while TV cameramen on board filmed a globe with pulsating lights, also seen by ground radar. Two UFOs, one a "spinning sphere with lateral lines surrounding it" were filmed on the return flight. Jet fighters were later put on full alert to intercept further UFOs.

1979, April. Cosmonaut Victor Afanasyev saw a "structured" UFO turn towards his spacecraft and follow it. The object "was an engineering structure, made from some type of metal, approximately 40 meters long with inner hulls. The object was narrow here and wider there, and inside there were openings. Some places had projections like small wings," he said.

1979, November. Forestry worker Bob Taylor came across a large gray circular object hovering just off the ground in a clearing in woods at Dechmont Law, Scotland. From it two spheres with spikes like naval mines rolled out and tried to pull him to it. He passed out and, when he came to they had all gone. He staggered a mile back home. He is considered a reliable witness by friends.

1980, April. Commandante Oscar Santa Maria Huertas of the Peruvian Air Force was sent up to intercept an unidentified "balloon" in restricted airspace near La Joya AFB, Arequipa, Peru. At 8,000 feet he fired a burst of shells at it but with no effect. The UFO ascended rapidly but he pursued it, sometimes at supersonic speed. Despite further lock-ons the UFO evaded him three more times by rapid ascent, eventually to 63,000 feet. This was not a balloon but a shiny dome-shaped wingless object.

1980s. In and above the Hessdalen Valley in Norway unusual lights in the sky have been reported since the 1940s. Bright white or yellow lights of unknown origin hovering or floating silently have been seen, sometimes for over an hour. High activity occurred in 1982 and 1983 and there has been much scientific research done to explain the lights, so far without convincing results. Some "structured craft" have also been seen.

1981, January. Trans-en-Provence, France. A UFO landed in the yard of a house and quickly took off, stirring up dust as it flew away. A nearby witness saw four openings on its underside.

1981, May. Russian Major General Vladimir Kovalyonok saw a UFO "that defied known laws of physics." Russia cosmonaut Alexandr Baladin is also on record as stating that flying saucers were seen close to the MIR space station.

1982, October. A cellular biology researcher in Nancy, France, observed a small shiny craft descend from the sky and hover just one meter above the ground in his garden for 20 minutes. Then it rapidly rose straight upward until it was lost to sight. The tips of the leaves of an amaranth plant near where it hovered were completely dried up as if by a very strong electric field.

1982, November. Portuguese Air Force pilot Julio Guerra flying near Torres Vedras, saw a metallic disk, 8-10 feet in diameter close to his Chipmunk plane at high speed. It performed a series of maneuvers including repeated orbits around his plane, coming to within 15 feet. Two other pilots arrived and saw it before it left.

1983, March. Ed Burns of IBM was driving north on the Taconic Parkway in New York State when he saw a huge craft, triangular in shape with 40 colored lights along its trailing edge alone, almost hovering over his car. It was moving very slowly. "This was a flying city. It was not a small craft. It was huge."

1983, October. Jim Cooke watched a huge silent triangular craft hover just 15 feet over Croton Falls reservoir, New York, for 15 minutes. Nine red lights on it came on and it seemed to be probing the water with a red beam or instrument that projected downward. When cars passed the lights would fade until the UFO was nearly invisible. Then the craft lifted upward and drifted slowly away into the night sky.

1984, July. A huge unidentified object shaped like an ice cream cone and "as big as three football fields" hovered over Indian Point Nuclear Plant near Buchanan, New York. It had eight bright lights on it and moved slowly above the complex to within 30 feet of a working reactor. A request was made for a National Guard armed helicopter to shoot it down but the UFO departed.

1986, November. Kenju Terauchi, captain of a Boeing 747 cargo jet, Japan Airlines Flight 1628, flying near Anchorage, Alaska, saw a gigantic round object with colored lights flashing along a horizontal rim. The UFO was as big as an aircraft carrier and flew on the same course as the 747 for 30 minutes. It was tracked by ground radar and seen by the 747's other two crew members. This and a second object stopped at one point in front of the 747 emitting heat which Terauchi could feel on his face.

1987-1990. Gulf Breeze, Florida, building contractor Ed Walters claimed various encounters with UFOs which he filmed over three years. Although many think he faked his pictures, there were undoubtedly real UFO sightings in this area at the time. Groups of watchers regularly saw a red glowing UFO, nicknamed Bubba, high in the sky over the Gulf of Mexico shoreline.

1988, January. The Knowles family of Nullarbor Plain, Australia, reported a UFO trying to lift their car off the road, along with strange "voice distortion." Nearby truck drivers also saw a UFO, as did tuna fishermen, 50 miles away, who also suffered from the same odd voice distortion during their close encounter

1989, February. Hundreds, if not thousands, of people witnessed a huge cylindrical object fly over the city of Nalchik in the Transcaucasus, Russia, at an altitude of less than 5000 feet. It traveled at 65 mph, was metallic and about 1,500 feet long with nose lower than its tail. It appeared to have spotlights front and back and "portholes." As it turned before flying away, fins were seen on its tail but these vanished when the turn was complete. This polymorphism was noted with other UFO cases in Russia.

1989, July. Kapustin Yar, army missile base, Russia. Seven military witnesses saw three objects that also seemed to be one brightly lit saucer, "hovering over the military unit [including a rocket weapons depot] for over an hour" and evaded, by very rapid motion, a fighter aircraft sent to investigate. The UFO shone beams of light into the base and changed shape to a triangle. It could move very quickly, yet "instantly stop in the air."

1990, March. Pereslavl-Zalesskiy, east of Moscow. Colonel-General of Aviation Igor Maltsev, Chief of Staff of the Air Forces, stated that a huge disk-shaped object picked up on radar "... rotated around its axis and performed an 'S-turn' flight both in the horizontal and vertical planes" in silence. It flew between 300 and 24,000 feet and was two to three times faster than a modern jet.

1990, August. At Calvine, Pitlochry, Scotland, a large diamond-shaped UFO was seen by witnesses hovering for 10 minutes next to an RAF Harrier, before shooting skyward. Photographs of the craft were analyzed by the MOD, whose Nick Pope said they showed a "solid-structured craft" about 25m in diameter.

1990. Cosmonaut Victor Gennadij Strekhalov aboard MIR Space Station saw a UFO. "I called Gennady Monaco ... to come to the porthole ... suddenly a kind of sphere appeared. Beautiful, shiny and glittering, I saw it for 10 seconds ... a perfect sphere."

1991, April. Alitalia pilot Achille Zaghetti reported a cigar-shaped UFO flying past his plane at high speed during descent to Heathrow Airport on a flight from Milan to London. Immediately following this near-miss, Zaghetti contacted the radar control, which confirmed an unidentified target was observed about 11 miles behind the plane. Ministry of Defence officials ruled out a missile, but offered no explanation for the sighting.

1991, May. At Pyatigorsk in the Russian Caucasus four bus company executives saw an enormous UFO accompanied by five fiery globes each with a small tail. Another large craft the size of a football pitch appeared with a huge nozzle at its center. Totally silent, this UFO stayed visible for a minute and then vanished.

1991. September. Jerinaldo Dantes, living on a farm in Rio Grande do Norte, Brazil, was bicycling home when a large multi-colored ball of light came after him. Frightened, he hid under a tree over which the UFO hovered giving out intense heat for about 20 minutes. He scrambled under a fence as the tree cracked and fell. The menacing blue light hovered over the stump, then left.

1992, April. George Wingfield observed a small white disk sailing silently through a cloudless blue sky thousands of feet above the Washington Monument. Behind it flew perhaps seven tiny pinpricks of light. Two female companions also saw the daylight disk and one took a photo of it. After some minutes the objects receded in the distance and were lost to view. Further objects were seen changing direction in the sky. They brightened, then vanished. Ten minutes later another dark shape-changing object flew silently and horizontally on a different course. "None of these UFOs were like an aircraft or other familiar object. This extraordinary flypast seemed almost surreal, yet all of us were sober and wide awake. This demonstrates something of the nature of the UFO phenomenon. Like some psychic apparition, these objects, whose actual physical existence was in no way provable, had somehow penetrated into our reality on that day."

1994, June. At Arad in Romania a shepherd, Traian Crisan, saw a circular craft some 3 meters above a wheat field at 4 a.m. A powerful blast of air knocked him down and blew off his hat. His sheep fled. The UFO had a small open door in which stood two figures with beards and mustaches, one just like an Orthodox Church priest. Then the UFO flew upward and departed leaving behind a large 42 meter crop circle.

1994, September. Teachers and school officials at the Ariel School in Ruwa, Zimbabwe, were amazed when about 60 school pupils, aged between 5 and 12 years old, reported that a flying object had landed on the school grounds. They saw strange beings emerge from the landed craft(s) of whom they later drew pictures. After 15 minutes the "spaceships" and entities faded from view.

1994. Chinese farmer Meng Zhaoguo from Wuchang saw a metallic shimmering on a mountain side. When he went to see he blacked out and later was visited by a ten-foot-high female alien. She was naked from the waist down and had 12 fingers. Meng says they had sex while levitating for about 40 minutes. The aliens told him that this would produce a hybrid child 60 years from now. He passed a police lie detector test.

2000, January. In different locations near Highland, Illinois, five on-duty police officers reported a huge unidentified triangular craft in the night sky. The object moved very slowly at times and also at great speed without making any sound. Many other witnesses said the UFO had "very bright" or "blinding" lights. It flew in the area for up to 9 hours between 1000 feet and 2000 feet.

2000, May. Police inspector Kriel of Warden, South Africa, reported an oval-shaped UFO as wide as four lanes of the freeway. After two close approaches to his car, the object, equipped with a dome-like structure on top and beneath, moved away.

2001, April. An extremely bright circular UFO descended from the sky over a nuclear plant near Levice, Slovakia. It passed over an area where a nuclear pile had recently been closed and flew towards a facility that had just been made active. Narrowly missing two tall smokestacks it stopped over the first of 4 nuclear reactors. A TV news report said the UFO hovered just 20 feet over the active unit for 10 minutes before leaving.

2004, June. The U.S.AF noticed a number of UFOs rising from the ocean around Antarctica and sent up fighter jets. The UFOs disappeared from radar screens, reappeared where they had left the sea, and promptly dived back beneath the waves. Silvery disk-shaped UFOs were also seen by a pilot over Antarctica in 1952.

2006, November. A number of witnesses including United Airline pilots saw a metallic-looking disk hovering at about 1,500 feet over Gate C17 of Chicago's O'Hare airport below a cloud bank at 1,900 feet. It was observed for between 5 and 15 minutes. Then it shot upward at high speed leaving a clearly defined circular hole in the clouds through which blue sky could be seen.

2007, April. Captain Ray Bowyer flying a Trislander aircraft at 4,000 feet to Alderney in the British Channel Islands saw two huge brilliant yellow UFOs in the sky about 55 miles away, shaped like thin cigars but with a dark band around their right end. Both must have been about a mile long and were picked up on ground radar. The UFOs were also seen by the passengers.

2007, November. Witnesses in Dudley, West Midlands, UK, saw a silent, black triangle-shaped object in the sky like "a huge Dorito with distinctive red lights on its underside." Reappeared 2010.

2008, January. In Stephenville, Texas, a police officer tracked a huge UFO flying at low level with his radar speed gun. "I had to swivel my radar head up into the sky. And I knew I got a good hit on it. It showed 27 miles per hour and was accelerating slowly ... I want people to know that the citizens are telling the truth ..."

2008, June. A wave of UFO sightings in Wales included a police helicopter following a "flying saucer-shaped" UFO that had swooped down over it, above MOD St. Athan, an RAF base. The three-man crew pursued the brightly lit craft over the Bristol Channel until they ran low on fuel.

2009, January. A strike by a UFO apparently caused the 65-foot-blade of a wind turbine to break off (see page 55). The 290-foot-high turbine was severely damaged during the night at a wind farm near Conisholme, Lincs, UK, at a time when there had been several UFO sightings in the immediate area. A woman motorist was among dozens who saw flashing orange lights near the wind farm shortly before the smash. No satisfactory explanation has been produced.

2009, July 21st. The Russian navy declassified its UFO records. Svobodnaya Pressa reported 50% of UFO cases involved oceans and in once case a nuclear-powered submarine detected six unknown objects following it. Unable to shake them off, it rose to the surface and the objects did the same before flying off.

2009, October. RMCC Observatory, Mounds, Oklahoma. Five astronomers saw a shape-changing UFO with a group of lights rotating around its lower portion. The object shot out of sight at a speed that was "without question way beyond anything that we have knowledge of or is publicly known to be in our military."

2010, July. China's Xinhua news agency reported that after an unidentified flying object was spotted, airport officials stopped passengers from boarding planes, and outgoing flights were grounded for an hour in Hangzhou. Incoming flights were rerouted. No explanation has been offered, though several hours before the incident, many Hangzhou residents described seeing a large, brightly lit, elongated object in the sky.

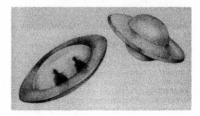